A Manifesto for equality & fairness in policing

Z Phillips

Published by New Generation Publishing in 2023

Copyright © Zoe Phillips 2023

First Edition

The author asserts the moral right under the Copyright, Designs and Patents Act 1988 to be identified as the author of this work.

All Rights reserved. No part of this publication may be reproduced, stored in a retrieval system or transmitted, in any form or by any means without the prior consent of the author, nor be otherwise circulated in any form of binding or cover other than that which it is published and without a similar condition being imposed on the subsequent purchaser.

ISBN: 978-1-83563-016-7

www.newgeneration-publishing.com

This book is dedicated to my late mother who was persistently abused by a violent husband yet would still have taken him back, after he left the family home when I was 11 years old. It is dedicated to every strong woman who has been abused by the law and who I have met, who have shared their sad stories with me – Veronica, Kim, Mital, the Caribbean lady who has painted my nails and to Zayna Iman who gave me the strength to eventually speak up about this. It's dedicated to the Women's Equality Party, Sky News and to Elainea Emmott who made the world stop and listen to us. It's dedicated to men who want to change the system. It's dedicated to each of you that helped me through this – you all know who you are. Apologies if I have not listed you individually, but here are a few: David, Peter, Geoffrey, Jean, Mary, Anna, Charlotte H and Charlotte A, Claire, Lou, Marie, Michael, Mark A. Most of all, this book is written for and dedicated to all of you who read it, to protect you and ensure that this never happens to you but if it does, it will not take 3.5 years out of your life to find out what to do.

"If one day something changes in your heart and for some reason you stop loving my daughter, please don't hurt her, bring her back to me".

#thebigberyl 2023

Contents

Relationship red flags	3
An arrest	7
At the Station	14
Being released from the police station	21
Once Home	27
Who to ask or where to go for help/what to do next:	31
The Court	36
After the plea hearing	46
The implications of pleading guilty	50
The appeal process	51
References	57
Vocabulary	58
Charities and Organisations	60
Parliamentary Ministers	62
The Courts and levels	63

Thank you for choosing to read this book.

It is intended to assist anyone who finds themselves in a position you would never have dreamt you would be in, in a million years. I am hoping that through my experience, I can offer advice and point out red flags within relationships, within the police and within the system. I have tried to include advice that I did not know at the time but have found out subsequently through endless subject access requests, data on file requests via the ICO and after I have submitted 47 heads of complaints about the MET Charing Cross Police to the IOPC and MOPAC, not to mention complaints to the legal ombudsman about the law firm that abandoned me 7 working days prior to a trial and a barrister that told me to change my plea 36 hours prior to the trial (after 7 months of pleading not guilty) so that I could do the court a favour and because I would be committing a crime by having my accuser cross examined, despite his bad behaviour towards me. I have also learned some aspects having complained to IPSO, the press standards authority about why my case was covered so sensationally before a trial, where they got the information from and why it was covered when no journalist was present in court. I have also been through the appeal process for the last 1,196 days of my life and counting. Most importantly, I want to help give you the inner strength to know how, when and with what to stand up for yourself if you are not guilty and have had lies told against you to have you arrested.

Relationship red flags

If a partner starts to gas light[1] a former partner, eg. "she emotionally destroyed me", "she is an evil bitch" this is a **red flag**. Question it. One day, he may use the same adjectives and phrases about you and not just on a WhatsApp text message to his new girlfriend, but to the police.

- Beware of phrases he uses in text message stating that he's realised he "needs help" or is having to "cope with booze".
- Find out about the partner, if he's been divorced, why and was it acrimonious?
- Does he have children and is he still a part of their life?
- NB If he mentions he has 1 daughter when you meet and you subsequently find out he has 2, red flag.
- If a partner forces himself on you, insists that you turn to face the wall (it doesn't need to be 3 times) whilst he uses anything other than his genitals to penetrate you, this

is RAPE[2] this is not only coercive control, any reasonable person would realise that this creates a hostile environment and that his behaviour is not just criminal but has violated your dignity

- It is now your choice to report him or not.

REPORT him to the police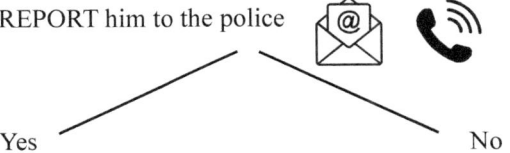

Yes

- The perpetrator will most definitely retaliate
- Do not email him to let him know you reported him
- Be prepared to be accused of having harassed him, his new partner or similar
- Consider wisely whether you wish to make a statement, but better do this soon because if he makes a counter complaint and you are arrested, the police could refuse your ability to make a full statement as they may state in writing that they prefer his narrative
- Know that you are in this for the long term, it will not be a quick process

No

- Walk away from this relationship
- At least withdraw from contact
- If you share the same social circle, stay strong and prepare for meeting him again
- He will probably do this to someone else – let them decide whether to report him or not

1. *If* you are allowed to make a statement about rape, it will be a video statement
2. It could take as much as 5 months to interview him as the police tell you "for protection of his privacy"
3. Expect him to retaliate and accuse you of something else within days, for which, however menial, you will be charged
4. Ask the police when you and he will be advised of the outcome of the investigation – you should be told simultaneously, not 4 weeks after he is told

An arrest

It's not something we anticipate, are brought up to know about, nor to expect especially if you are a normal, law-abiding citizen of the United Kingdom, but if it happens, consider the following:

- If a counter complaint has been made to your initial complaint, neither party should be arrested according to the Police College code of conduct* (PACE code). It is unlawful to summarily arrest either party.

- The police have options before spending time, money and resource on physically arresting you. Demand to know the full reason as to why your arrest is needed. Their options include but are not limited to:

    o Initial warning about the accusation made about you

    o An invitation to the station for an interview under caution

    o A physical arrest (by any number of

officers depending on what situation they think they will walk into)

- o If you had already made a report about the accuser, ensure you mention that you did and wish to make a full statement which you were unsure about making in the first place (and if you do have a discussion with the police officer, specify if you want a female officer especially if rape was involved and also follow up to obtain a copy of any body video footage that the officer may have taken whilst at your meeting place)

- A balance of male and female officers should be lawfully present at a physical arrest, not 4 male officers to arrest a single female from an apartment she lives in alone. It's disproportionate and shows inequality. In this day and age, it is unacceptable for a single woman to be seized by 4 men. Point this out to them.

- If 4 male officers arrive at your front door at midnight, shining lights through windows, and you are a woman living alone, this is unacceptable. The police shifts normally end at midnight or around that time, so they could arrest you at 7am the following morning, it will make no difference to them but a big difference to you because your case will NOT be looked at until the morning shift start and they arrive at their desks at about 8.30am the following morning anyway.

- If there is a global pandemic, police officers should be wearing masks, they should ask you if you have symptoms and they should also insist that you wear a mask particularly when being put inside a police van, however large. If they do not do this, point it out to them.

- Every step you take, and they take, and every word you say will be on camera (all police officers wear a BMV - a body worn video). Ensure you ask for this immediately afterwards as they may choose to 'delete it' after 7 days and then it is lost evidence for you.

- Do NOT say 'sorry what have I done' do not say 'SORRY' at all. Sorry will be translated in all police records as "I admit that I am guilty". You are not guilty until proven guilty, despite any police behaviour to the contrary. No matter how much the police try to make you feel, you are NOT guilty if you are simply NOT guilty and you have evidence to show a relationship, and malicious messages and the reasons why you reported that person in the first place.

- When being arrested and they ask you to put on suitable clothing to be taken to the station, wear anything preferably without a cord or any type of 'trim' (eg. Fur etc) on a jacket. Do not wear big winter boots. Despite the police having frog marched you out of the house and knowing this, they will let you wear these clothes and then force you to remove all of the above and put on prison clothing. Also, be ready for them to rip the 'trim' off the jacket, whether it is meant to be removed or not.

- If you are asked to put clothes on in your apartment before you leave, maintain privacy. It is not acceptable for 4 male officers to demand that you leave the door ajar 5-6 inches, so they can "check on you".

- If you are asked to change at the station, ask for a private area (they usually have a 'shower' of sorts which offers a modicum of privacy). If you change in a cell, know that you are on CCTV and the rest of the police officers will be watching you on their screens in the 'check in' area and probably laughing at you, especially if you were rushed to put clothing on and had no time to put on any underwear underneath your personal clothing.

- Know that watches, computers, and your mobile 'phones will be seized and placed in sealed plastic bags. If possible, always remember the telephone number of a family member (if they are still alive) or a close friend you can confide in. You will be able to let the police make one call on your behalf when in your cell, to advise someone where you are. The call will be relayed to your cell via a loudspeaker in the wall of the cell.

- Once in the cell, you will have no notion of the time of day or night as there are no windows and no clocks just a fluorescent strip light, a wooden bench, a thin blue mattress, a thin matted blue blanket, one roll of loo paper of the greaseproof-paper kind and a loo with no seat. Oh, and a camera to observe your every move. It is not the Ritz.

- Be sure to advise them if you have any medical issues – epilepsy, asthma, diabetes, heart failure, to mention a few critical illnesses. The arrest experience is hugely stressful and your body may throw you into a clinical situation you had not anticipated with the trauma. Be sure to take enough medications to cover you for at least 24 hours (the maximum time the police are allowed to hold you in a prison cell).

- Do not attempt to take a bottle of water with you on arrest. The police will sniff it and confiscate it. They can provide you with tepid tap water in polystyrene cups in the cell when you ask for water (via a buzzer in the wall of your cell – NB. Don't expect this to be answered immediately and don't forget that the police officer at the end of this buzzer can mock you and be rude and you will never know his name, rank or what he looks like. The police might consider it their prerogative to goad you and make you even more distressed, annoyed and upset). Try to ignore and remain calm. Breathe deeply.

- Do not expect much in the way of food. It is usually pre-packed biscuits thrown through the hole in your cell door (with a cover slid across from outside the cell) as well as the tap water.

- From the moment you are arrested, be prepared that how you react and what you say will impact your future, personally and professionally in every way.

At the Station

- In the 'check in' area, you will be allowed your mobile 'phone back for 5 minutes, to take down 4-5 'phone numbers of friends or family (if you are lucky enough to have any left). If you have a friend who is a lawyer, this would be useful, although do not be surprised if that person does not answer, try the next one on your list. And be careful if the person you choose knows the accuser (you do not know if he may have used them as a witness). NB. Once you are put through to someone and you speak, this is your one and only call for however long you will be in that cell, so use it wisely with someone you trust.

- Know that this may be the last time you see your 'phone for 5 months (the law states the police can keep it for this long, even apparently if it has evidence on which you need for your defence).

- Do not try to be nice or forgiving about your accuser (especially if it is your ex-partner). Know that you have not been arrested by 4 male officers because he said he didn't like you very much anymore. Know that in a statement he has made, he WILL have lied, distorted the truth and fabricated many stories about you (unless you are of course some sort of horrendous 'bunny boiler' in which case, you deserve to be incarcerated). He will state things like "I never stayed the night at her flat" "I didn't know her" etc vs your evidence. It will be extraordinarily exaggerated. Do NOT be surprised (you did see the text messages and vocabulary he sent you about the girl before you...it will be no surprise that this will be the language he has used against you). Do not feel empathy for that person at all. You may be a natural 'resolver' but do NOT try to fix things and appease the situation in a police station or at interview. Do NOT say SORRY for anything.

- Ask for a duty solicitor immediately (unless you happen to have your own contacts) otherwise these people can take 8-9 hours to arrive to 'represent' you. Keep asking where this person is if you have not spoken with a lawyer, anything you say or do not say could be used against you before you speak to a lawyer.

- When you are given a duty solicitor and he/she says they will represent you, ask for their card immediately so you have their contact details. You do not have a notepad and pen in a cell and nothing to record any information and you will not be able to remember details like this as you will be in such shock.

- Most importantly, ask for evidence that they are a practising lawyer. The SRA (Solicitors' Regulation Authority) will confirm this afterwards. If they are not able to validate this, be suspicious. If you eventually discover that their licence was terminated years ago, complain. You have the right to have the interview erased as inappropriate evidence not just because you were in such a state of shock.

- Beware if the duty solicitor advises: "just say sorry you won't do it again". Again, refer to my point, do NOT say "SORRY" for anything you have NOT done. Do not think it will just speed things up so you will be released. If anything, it will extend your time in that cell.

- If you had not harassed anyone (know the

accusation and the point of law you have allegedly broken) state that you had not. If you had responded to his emails even in self-defence, state this. Be prepared that an ex-partner will make anything up to coerce everyone into believing he had done nothing wrong and that you are the criminal. Be prepared that none of his 100's of loving, sweet and lovely text messages to lead you on will be mentioned in his statement, he will not have been nice about you at all. Know this. Do not make excuses for him or take on the blame for his erratic and emotionally abusive behaviour.

- You have the right to ask for another responsible adult to be present. You may be 15 or 50, but ask for this. You do need it if you've never been in this situation before and it is the law if you ask for it, for them to provide it on top of your duty solicitor. They will offer moral support if nothing else. If you are not offered it, this is another reason that the interview could be discarded.

- Once in a cell, you are allowed to make one 'phone call via the in-cell 'intercom' speaker built into the wall of the cell.

Make it count. Think before you call as to what you will say. Be prepared, and not just utterly floored by the whole situation, and by no means ask that person, once you get through to someone, to step in, to talk sense to your ex-partner and try to free you. You will be re-arrested in the cell before you know it and unbelievably, this could be a whole new arrest, charge, court case and ultimately a conviction against you for having 'perverted the course of justice' or attempted to.

- You may be told you need to be interviewed by the 'police mental health nurse'. Do not joke about having considered taking your life due to the stress of the ex-partner, as they will record you as a danger to yourself and others. Do say you don't want to and do not need to be interviewed by this nurse and DO ask them NOT to put this on your GP records. You have this option, but **only if you ask** for it not to be sent to your GP – otherwise it will be on your medical records forever, proof that you had been arrested and taken into custody even if it was only 12.5 hours or 17.5 hours. This will impact your job opportunities in the future, forever.

Even if you have never taken one mental health medication in your life and you have never been referred to a psychiatrist for formal mental health help, they will categorise you as mentally unstable in all police documentation that they keep forever. It will be traumatic and take years (10+) to try to have this information cleared on all their records when you know it is not correct, appropriate or fair.

- NB. It is wrong for the police to suggest that just because you are from a broken home, that you must be a criminal. Ignore them, do not let it phase you. It's just another way of them goading you into believing that you must be a bad person because of someone else's fault. If you have not done or sent anything threatening, violent, vindictive or abnormal, (in this case of alleged 'harassment without violence') but replied to your accuser, then why are you being called a criminal? Your parents splitting up should NOT be used by the police to define who you are in law or in life.

- And remember to obtain a full transcript as soon as possible of your full interview because the police summary WILL have errors in it and will be written to classify you as guilty.

- You have the right to know if a friend has visited you whilst you were in the cell. It is against the human rights act for the police to withhold this information and for the visitor to have been told you were asleep in your cell when this was blatantly not true and data on file shows you were, at the time, being interviewed by the prison mental health nurse.

Being released from the police station

- The police can retain you for 24 hours in a cell, so be prepared to stay for a long time. If you have been arrested in the daytime, know that you may be released in the middle of the night and if this is in January, it will be cold and possibly raining or snowing. Your mind and body will also be in shock. You will probably be uncontrollably shaking.

- If you need to use the bathroom before you leave, ask to do so. If you need Tampax or sanitary towels, ask a female police officer for them. Your body will be in shock and you do not know what will happen. You may start spontaneously haemorrhaging. I did. In torrents. It was the last menstruation of my life. I will never have my own child.

- If you can afford it, take a taxi home. Ask for a police vehicle, though they are more likely to say there is no one available to drive you, even if there are plenty of vehicles in their car park. You will not be driven back to your home by the police.

- Ask for your things back. Clothes, jewellery, watches, handbag, wallet, oyster card, everything. The police will have emptied the contents of a purse, so do check it is all there when you get it back. You can ask for your computers and mobile 'phones back but do not anticipate getting any of those items back. [The police can hold onto these to investigate evidence for up to 5 months. This could work to your advantage as they could have seen your evidence for themselves – however know that they will most probably never open them, just leave them in the sealed plastic bags they put them in when they arrested you, your evidence remaining untouched, disregarded and discarded NB. Against the police actions, this is an obstruction of justice and a failure to disclose evidence – if your case goes to court].

- Ask for your work equipment back. Force this point. Especially if it has nothing but work matters on it. Tell the police you need your work equipment for your livelihood. The police may suggest that you lie to your employer by telling them the equipment was stolen. Do not. Especially if you are innocent, explain fully to your manager at work. Any decent employer who respects you, needs you in the organisation and knows you add value, will, if anything, support you through this. They may even be able to demand the return of the equipment via their in-house lawyers, for corporate security reasons. [NB. If your employer gives you a veiled threat, start to seek employment elsewhere as soon as possible before they make you resign stating you have committed a gross misconduct by being arrested.].

- If you are released at 01:00hrs, there might be night buses if you live in London, but that's different in other parts of the country. Don't be alone. You will be traumatised and not really functioning properly, plus you might have sudden medical issues. Police stations are not often located in the most salubrious parts of town and sometimes have various vagrants around them attending food banks or dealing drugs. A London black cab driver is also a good listener usually as you will not believe what just happened – and nor will they. Clearly ordering an online taxi will not be possible as you will not have a 'phone. Safety is your issue here, get home safely.

- Ask the police officer discharging you for a contact email, to continue to ask for your digital devices back. But be warned, that officer will be representing the accuser, not you. Anything you ask them, even if it's whether you can visit a particular club or not, will be reported back to the accuser. They will NOT be looking after your best interests. Do not apologise for anything, do not say SORRY but you will need these contact details because this person will be inviting you back to the station to 'charge' you 2 weeks later or so, if they do decide to charge you (even if someone has committed suicide having been through the very same process only days prior to this happening – Caroline Flack). This police officer will be the one deciding to escalate the case to the CPS (Criminal Prosecution Service). Once you are in this system, there is no going back, nothing you can do to stop descending into the black hole of the British Criminal Justice system. Your life will change forever. You will not be believed by friends or family, you will lose your job, your life as you knew it, your civil liberties, your money, your accommodation to name a few norms of life.

- NB. When the dust settles over your case, unfortunately most probably once you have been found or pleaded guilty, ask for data on file. It may take 2 years to obtain this data, but you might well discover that a senior officer had stated that the accusation against you did not reach the threshold to go to the CPS. This is important in an appeal, especially if it had escalated and you had been charged, because someone or something changed the instructions.

- Data on file will also reveal whether the police were given any "special instructions" on how to handle you (by a particularly malicious accuser and/or his new partner).

- NB. If his new partner is also carrying his child, be aware that her emotions will be running high and she is likely to go to extreme lengths to defend the father, your ex-partner. NB. Also know that the CPS have guidelines on how to treat pregnant women. (Equal Treatment Bench Book -

February 2021 (judiciary.uk)). They can be excused from cross examination in a court room. Know this, because although this person could have been used as your accuser's witness, she may not even be cross-examined on her sworn statement on trial day, even if you know she also lied on oath to frame you.

- The police officer releasing you will most probably give you a free 4-page leaflet with the telephone number of Samaritans on it. Use it and keep it in a safe place for the start of your journey through this.

Once Home

If you are on your own, try to stay calm.

Stay strong.

Call Samaritans if you have a landline.

Think logically and be organised

1. Do you have an old mobile 'phone handset? Get it out and take this to a mobile 'phone shop in the morning where you can buy a temporary £10 SIM card and set up a temporary number. If the following morning is a Sunday, remember the shop may not be open until late and only for a few hours. Remember the police and your ex-partner chose the time to arrest you to provide maximum inconvenience to you and your normal life, scheduled travel plans or routines. [NB. If you had not blocked your ex-partner, remember that he is probably stalking your every move online to know where you are and when – in the future,

this may work against you as he and the CPS may demand court hearings when you are out of the country].

2. NB. If you have a WhatsApp account, open the app on this old 'phone. Some of your contacts may still be on the 'phone. [NB. Be sure to perform a 'chat back up' regularly on your devices, especially if you have evidence to contradict the accusations being thrown at you. They will not all reappear on the new device, but you might be lucky and get some back. Remember that your ex-partner will have deleted any evidence to show the two of you had any sort of relationship].

3. On any mobile device, make sure you save contacts to the handset as well as the number. You need this evidence when it is returned to you.

4. Do you have a very old computer or can you borrow one as soon as possible? [NB. The police will 'sweep' your flat of any digital equipment when they arrest you. Do check their warrants though – if questioned, they may NOT have the authority to seize any equipment, ask. They are unlikely to seize old equipment

that does not work unless it's plugged in and has not been used in over 10 years. Dig this out, plug it in and pray that it will still work. It is your lifeline]. Hopefully, your Facebook and social profiles will still be available, and you can privately message people to let them know your new SIM card number and the reasons why. Friends may also be lovely and understand the situation stating that "you can vent with them".

5. But be prepared that some 'friends' may betray you and some will not want to know you at this juncture and drop all contact. It's difficult if you are alone and more difficult if isolated due to any global pandemic. Stay strong, calm and nurture those relationships which are true to you and helpful. Do NOT listen to anyone who says "just plead guilty and get it over with" if that does not fit well with you, do not be persuaded to admit to anything you are not guilty of even if they think they are being helpful.

6. If you were due to go away on the day you were arrested, try to rearrange flights as soon as possible and email the hotel to ask them to keep your room, you just missed

a night. Go away on your holiday or work commitment if it was booked already. It is the best thing to do after this experience, as long as the police have not taken your passport.

Who to ask or where to go for help/what to do next:

- Do ask any friends you have who are lawyers if you can confide in them and ask for what they recommend. They may not operate in criminal law but if they are a friend, they will do their best to help. Being a lawyer, they will keep the information confidential. You need a friend onside and who actually believes you and believes in you.
- Be prepared to start to pay £1,000's of pounds to defend yourself immediately.
- Don't just accept this advice and google search 'what do I do if I have been arrested' or any other information. This will presumably give you some advice and also direct you to appropriate law firms at all cost levels.
- Do ask the lawyer you hire to estimate what it will cost you. No use hiring a lawyer to whom you pay £16,500, leaving you destitute after 7 months of paying

them only to leave you unable to find a further £8,000 they demand, giving you a 5-day deadline to find this, to pay them to represent you at a trial days later. NB. Usually criminal lawyers need money on account in order to represent you, if you cannot pay them up front, they write to court to state they do not represent you anymore and you can do nothing about it. You can ask if they would consider a payment plan, but most criminal lawyers do not offer this. There are 'direct access' barristers which will be less expensive than hiring a solicitor, but only a few operate like this in complicated cases and they are unlikely to take a case on if they only have 7 working days to prepare to represent you and prepare to cross examine the accuser. Forecast the amount this will cost you. [This may be difficult because if the accuser continues to make more allegations about you over 7 months of court hearings and the CPS demand weekly court hearings, then the costs will escalate rapidly].

- Charities like 'Advocate' or 'APPEAL' may be able to assist but charities can usually only handle a few cases and they are asked by hundreds of people. Again, don't leave this to the last minute as 'Advocate' state they cannot even consider your case if the trial is less than 3 weeks away. 'APPEAL' may consider representing you through an appeal process, not at the initial trial.

- If it is days prior to a trial that you are left without a lawyer, know that in the UK, the court might offer you a free-of-charge section 38 lawyer, to cross examine the accuser. I was unaware of this at the time and it's worth taking up their offer to do this if you are in a difficult financial situation.

- If you have no job, it's definitely worth asking for Legal aid. If you have a job, anything paid over £12,500 a year, you will not be allowed Legal aid. [NB. This is currently under review in the UK, as many middle income people find themselves having no money after months of paying lawyers to defend them].

- Consider representing yourself as a 'litigant in person', especially for relationship issues and certainly where there has been 'tit for tat' allegations and a clear counter claim retaliatory allegation.

You know the story best and you can do this. Never fear that you will not be able to do this.

- Once the CPS get involved, particularly if you have been physically arrested (the police decided that you needed to be, based on the narrative they had been given by your accuser), be prepared for a long and painful ride. In the PACE guidelines, it states that in counter allegations, neither party should be arrested to avoid bias by the CPS. If you are arrested, you are at an immediate disadvantage.

- Know that if your accuser has access to contacts and money, that they will pay for the best lawyers to spin the narrative in their favor, which will further work to your disadvantage and to discredit you.

- If the accuser's statement is over 100 pages in length, be suspicious. Has this person prosecuted someone in the past? Do they have form? Are they following a 'blueprint' and created the 'perfect case' to prosecute?

- Be aware that even if, in self-defence, you stated on a private text message or email, that you would 'rather die' than receive any further vindictive or malicious messages from him, your accuser will twist this to state you are 'suicidal'. There are no lengths an accuser like this will go to, to win the case against you. The moment 'suicide' is mentioned, the Police and CPS take this to a whole new level, assuming you are a danger to yourself and the public. Even if you sent it to him in defiance and indignation to ask him to stop sending further abusive messages. Know that nothing <u>you</u> sent was abusive or threatening.

The Court

- The first hearing may be 2-3 months after your arrest.
  When you arrive at the court, there will be press taking your photograph outside. Be prepared. You are a woman and creating a juicy story, even if not true sells papers. Condemning a woman sells their newspapers, particularly those akin to 'tittle tattle', such as the online Daily's. If you can, take a photograph of the journalist and ask who they represent. Confront them. You are able to confront anyone that takes a photograph of you without asking your permission. They will not like this and will probably not, as a result, publish any images of you. Every time I used this offensive, there was no press coverage. Be prepared as these press photographers usually have long lens cameras so you may not see them despite keeping an eye out for them. They also hide behind pillars or walls. They will not tell you where they work but give you the name of a UK general press agency. It could be anyone.

- Be prepared that in the press coverage, they will state your full name, age, address, companies you have worked for. They will make assumptions about your personal wealth and what you did. They will describe the outfit you are wearing and if astute will even name the brand.

- Be prepared that if there is press coverage online, it will gather a lot of hateful troll messages. Humans can be very cruel to other humans, particularly to females. The comments will be nasty, malicious and inhuman, be prepared, don't look it up, if you can help it. Ask a friend to take screen shots – you may need this later in the process to prove what you have been subjected to and the huge distress and damage to you that this has caused.

- Phrases such as "Never stick your wedge into crazy" is an example of a trolling message I received in response to the Press Coverage.

- Do take the full day off work for a court hearing and share the reason why with your manager. It's best to ask for their help and support all the way through this. Again, I am confident that any reasonable employer will support you, will not bully

about you. You will not have time to work through this. Aside from being in complete shock at someone you trusted having turned against you especially if he raped you, not the other way around. There will be too many allegations within it for you to break each down and prove that he had lied. Besides, the police have all your digital equipment, with all his messages and emails on, so you have no physical evidence to counter the claims.
- Let the CPS perform.
- Take a notebook into the 'dock' (a glass-sided room where the defendant sits or stands) and make as many notes as possible. Record key words or phrases or evidence he has used. Do not be shocked by anything, just write it down. You need to know what your ex-partner has stated, how he has created a very different narrative and therefore, what you are up against. He may have invented things such as 'stalking diaries' that you had no idea existed. Even if he claimed to have completed this during the time you were seeing each other, he will probably have downloaded it from the internet and completed it retrospectively. His

handwriting (the same style, size and ink) will be a sign to show that the bogus diary was completed at the same time at a later date.

- Be prepared for his new partner to corroborate with his story, especially if she is carrying his child and they are not married (he will reveal all these details in his statement). Even if you do not know who she is, have never met her and are not interested in her at all, be prepared that she knows all about you and has probably stalked all of your social media accounts. [NB. Recall his form in gaslighting his former partners].

- Be prepared for allegations such as you had been seen hanging around outside offices, homes etc. The CPS need CCTV to prove this and if none exists, this is a red flag. They are making you out to be someone you are not. Know that they will say anything to undermine you and create the notion that you are a danger to society. It is in their interests to make you out to have 'bad a character'.

- Know that if you have had any dealings with the police in the past, even reporting a break-in, or receiving a speeding fine, this will be on your file, and you will have a black mark against you. Again, as mentioned previously, this is very difficult to remove and sometimes is incorrectly recorded. It is good to obtain a Disclosure and Barring Service (DBS) certificate of yourself after the arrest to confirm to yourself, to the police and courts, that you have received no criminal convictions in the past and that you have no restraining orders. [NB. This is useful if the National Probation Service create their pre-sentence report and indicate that you have a previous criminal conviction, when you do not].

- Be prepared that his new partner may have sent out libellous emails to public organisations to further gaslight you to more people you know. She may have stated things in writing that you are "known to the police as a dangerous woman" which is untrue, suspiciously, the day before he made his statement to the police. [NB, The police advise that libel is a civil case and not criminal even though it has been used against you in a court of law. The police will treat you as if you have no rights in this regard. In their eyes, you are the perpetrator and he is the victim]. Before you know it, you will be labelled a scorned woman by more people than you can imagine. If you are sent any libellous emails or text messages from any source, keep them, save them and try to obtain data on file, a subject access release, from the organisation that was sent the libellous email. This is in line with the Information Commissioner's Office (ICO) where it provides you with a template to request this information.[4] Whilst some associations or people may suspiciously refuse to give you this information, ICO will do what they can to help. You can ask for libellous statements like the above to be deleted and for them to 'unblock' you if this had been actioned as a result of your accuser's control and influence over them. (This can include being dis-invited strangely, at the last minute, from charity events you had a ticket to, or text messages sent to organising committees to ask the association to 'red flag' you from events. Expect anything, your accuser will do anything he can to ensure that people believe his narrative).

- If you are not guilty, you are not guilty,

do not be swayed by any lawyer you have never met, who tells you to plead guilty to do everyone else a favour. You are NOT breaking the law by having your accuser cross examined. Under the Magna Carta, everyone has the right to a fair trial. You are NOT GUILTY.

- If you are highly persuaded to change your plea hours before the plea hearing but you still feel uncomfortable about this, state that in court at the plea hearing. State that you do not believe you are, but have been told to say 'guilty' by a new lawyer who does not know your case and has not considered the evidence. In that plea hearing, no matter what any lawyer tells you, state that the accuser lied and this is why you cannot plead 'guilty'. This is called an equivocal plea and if you wish to appeal your plea immediately afterwards, it is so important that you state this in court at the plea hearing. Tell the court that you have been told to plead guilty after spending 7 months pleading not guilty.

- Always ask whether all your accuser's witnesses are still witnesses – this may reveal that at least 1 of his witnesses had already stood down, which will undermine his case. Know that partners of an accuser may also be discredited as they are more likely to support their partner – some courts may discount their evidence. If they are pregnant this will be a motivating factor for them to support their partner. Ask about this.

- Clearly to do this, you must be confident that you have strong evidence that the accuser lied and that you are innocent and not guilty.
- Through data on file, you might be able to obtain the court notes. This may be useful later especially if the court did not record any plea at all. This is a mistake of process by the court.
- If you have not signed any indictment, nor any basis, such documents may also not be legally binding.

After the plea hearing

- If you pleaded guilty or are found guilty, the court will organise a 'sentencing' hearing at a later date. A sentence hearing will be when the court decide how badly to punish you. You will receive the criminal conviction. In addition, you may also be hit with a fine, court costs, compensation costs to the accuser (the alleged 'victims'), community service, a community order (when you need to visit a probation officer for the minimum number of 20 times over a 12 month period or longer, which comprises weekly visits to a probation office next to a prison) and as many restraining orders as your accuser negotiates with the police. It is unusual unless you are a murderer or are clearly guilty of a very bad crime, but you can be given this to last 'ad infinitum' ie. to last forever. Only through a whole appeal process can this length of time be reduced and even if the Crown Court agrees to reduce it to, for example, to 8 years, the accuser can still appeal this and demand that it be extended again. You are never out of this loop once in the system. You can ask for a reference from the probation officer that is allocated to you, but this is not a friend, all they will write is that you attended all the meetings, that is it. They are not interested in you as a good person with a previous blemish-free reputation. As a woman, you are also given access to 'Solace Women's aid' and Rape Crisis. You are categorised as an offender who needs help to stop reoffending so if you are not guilty, this is not an easy process to accept and follow.

- Prior to this hearing, the National Probation Service (NPS) are asked to write a 'Pre-Sentence Report' (PSR). Do not wait for them to call or contact you, you will need to contact them. Usually, they organise one telephone call between you and one of their officers. During this call, you are expected to state that you are remorseful for your crime. This one call usually lasts about an hour. [NB. If you are called, repeatedly, by one male probation officer, each time unscheduled and lasting over 1.5 – 2 hours, this is not normal. Complain to the NPS].

- Record each call so that you have evidence

of any probation officer mocking you and telling you that "all men behave badly, it's normal and you just have to accept it". It's inappropriate. It's also highly inappropriate that a probation officer judges your family in their report, for example by writing: "her father is a Reginald Perrin". Probation officers are not medically trained, so it is also inappropriate if the probation officer states that he thinks you are "emotionally unstable". This is not right nor fair. A PSR that is over 10 pages in length is also questionable, they are usually 1-2 pages in length. This is concerning.

- Always check these reports - if the probation officer has ticked a box that indicates you had a previous conviction when you had not, and you have had a clean DBS certificate all your life, this is incorrect and paints you in a bad light to the court. They will probably not amend it, but point it out. It's also not usual for a probation officer to call you after sentencing to say how surprised he was about your conviction and sentence.

- Keep all emails and save any correspondence with anyone about your case even those sent overnight. It's mandatory to be able to show that you made an equivocal and forced plea, and in impossible circumstances. when you were really not guilty.

The implications of pleading guilty

- Know that this will demonstrably change your life, negatively, as mentioned above.
- Know the difference between a conviction and a sentence. In certain circumstances, you might be able to appeal one, or both, but know the difference from the start. I didn't realise that 'the conviction' is everything, 'the sentence' is just the restraining orders, other add-on penalties and fines. It could also include a prison sentence.

The appeal process

It is infinitely more difficult to protest your innocence and show how wrong the process was, plus to show that lies were used to condemn you, if YOU plead guilty. I did not know that. If you're unsure yet you know in your heart you are not guilty and no one has seen the evidence, better to plead NOT guilty and appeal if you are found guilty, especially if lies had been used to convict you and you have strong evidence to show that these were lies which have never been considered by the police, CPS or court. Evidence which would undermine the prosecution case against you.

- A criminal record. This may remain on your police file until you die unless you quash it (ie. have it lifted). It means that you will have to disclose this on every job application, on any visa to travel with to certain countries in the world, in any diplomatic or defence attaché role you would be develop vetted for. It will be on your file. You may even be told to leave your accommodation on account of having a criminal record, even if you protest that it's not fair or right. It affects you personally and professionally forever.

- Whilst the conviction and the restraining orders are in place, the police, your ex-partner, a neighbour, a flat management company, anyone can and will use this against you in future and the police will have the power to arrest you spontaneously as you will be categorised 'a criminal'. Forget loans, mortgages, new bank accounts, moving abroad, and any other privilege of your civil liberties as a British citizen. So do not plead guilty unless you are.

- What are restraining orders - are they workable? What does indirect contact mean? You do have a right (apparently) to have this clarified otherwise, be warned that your ex-partner will use these as an excuse to have you re-arrested time and time again on any spurious grounds. This is difficult to work with if you've been in the same social circle for over 5 years. Make this clear to the court and to your legal counsel.

NB. As I write this book, I have subsequently discovered that if you contest anything to do with the case, the

CPS can accuse you of 'indirect contact' of your accuser, which though sounds ridiculous, apparently can be used against you too. You will have no voice and no right to an opinion at all.

The moral in this is NEVER plead guilty or be coerced to plead guilty for something you did not do.

- Be aware that if a former friend even mentions to him that you've been in touch, privately, as a friend, even when that friend had stated that you could vent with him, a particularly vindictive ex-partner may usurp this information off this person only to have you re-arrested and convicted of breaching your restraining order for this. If you are charged, you will end up back in court, any chance of an appeal will be thrown out and you may receive a prison sentence. [Perjury, (lying) is up to 5 years, but again, as you are considered the criminal, your accuser and anyone else that lied about you will be believed and you are not allowed to file a complaint of perjury as you are convicted.]

- The best thing to do is to continue to plead NOT guilty and no matter the stress, the distress, the pressure you are under, the circumstances, the fact your initial lawyer abandoned you, that you ran out of money, that you are in debt, that you've been told to leave your job, that it's a global pandemic, that you're alone and on your own going through all this, that you've been utterly besmirched by the press, that friends disown you and disassociate from you, nor any coercion by a fresh barrister that has no defence 'bundle', no 'cleanly collated evidence' to counter the lies and has not lived in your shoes for the previous 7 months, do NOT plead guilty.

- As I learned after the plea hearing, it probably would have been better for me to have asked the court for a section 36 or section 38 lawyer. A section 38 lawyer is free of charge and provided to you by the court. Not only will I have avoided any further costs, I could ill afford, but as I found out subsequently, a section 38 lawyer WILL cross examine the accuser, and will be present to represent you in a trial at which you can plead NOT guilty. Although you may not have much time to brief them on the case and provide the evidence, that lawyer might ask the court for more time to acquaint herself or himself with the case or, defend you in a not guilty plea. This lawyer may be taken more seriously by a court if they ask, on your behalf, for the trial to be adjourned. (ie. postponed), which will enable you to find a barrister who will be available fully for you on the day of a trial, and not dividing his time between your case and another case he's already working on. It will also enable you to save a bit more money to pay them or at least to have more time to collate your evidence in an appropriate manner to present to the court, for them to take into consideration to prove your innocence and that the case brought against you was just borne out of 'bad blood' and your accuser's desire to cover up the relationship he had with you whilst he was clearly in a relationship with a number of other women, and, to cover up his bad behaviour.

To summarise, I hope you are never in the situation I found myself in, not to mention having no idea about any of this at all, but if you do find yourself sadly in this position, I hope that this book helps you navigate the system and insist on your rights as a law-abiding British Citizen.

"They thought they'd buried me, but they didn't know that they had buried a seed"

    Elainea Emmet, photographer, campaigner and activist. August 2023

References:

1. Gaslight: **Gaslighting** is the subjective experience in which an Individual's perception of reality is repeatedly undermined or questioned by another person. This term, derived from the 1944 American film 'Gaslight' entered colloquial usage in the mid-2010s.

2. MET (Metropolitan Police) definition of rape: https://www.met.police.uk/advice/advice-and-information/rsa/rape-and-sexual-assault

The Ministry of Defence (MoD) has also now issued a publication entitled "Tackling Sexual offending in Defence Strategy. 2023"

4. ICO link for data on file:
Your right of access | ICO

* PACE Code of conduct link:
PACE Code C 2019 - GOV.UK (www.gov.uk)
Ask for a copy if you find yourself in custody.

Vocabulary that I have learned and is useful to understand:

Adjourn

Coercive Control

Conviction

CPS definition of harassment accessible online - 2 unwanted and unsolicited forms of contact (even if this is to respond to someone and even if your response is sent in self-defence)

Community service

Community order

Digital Rape [MET ref: digital penetration contrary to Section 2 of the Sexual Offences Act 2003]

Flying Monkeys

Gaslighting

Impact statement

Libel

Malicious messages

Narcissist

Paladin Stalking diary

Probation officer

Slander

Sentence

Trolling

Victim's Right to Review (VRR)

Charities and Organisations I reached out to:

ACAS

Advance Charity

APPEAL

BBC Radio 4 Woman's Hour

Care International

Casey Review

Centre for Women's Justice

Change

Citizen's advice bureau though they do not deal with criminal law

Employment Tribunal Courts

The Fawcett Society

Forewarned

Forward assist (because my ex-partner was and continues to be a serving miliary officer and as I am a veteran and a former long-term partner of an army officer)

Hacked Off

Headstrong counselling, accessed via your

General Practitioner

Heads together

Help counselling centre

Help through court (accessed at the Royal Courts of Justice, London)

Me Too

The Pitman College of Shorthand

Rape crisis

Salute Her

Samaritans

Solace Women's Aid

Stowe family law podcasts

South Westminster Legal Advice Centre (SWLAC)

Turn 2 Us

Women's Aid

Women International

Women's Equality Party (WEP)

Victim's support (via the Victim's Commissioner)

Parliamentary Ministers I connected with to ask to appeal my case:

The Prime Minister

The Chairman of the Conservative Party

The Policing Minister

The Victim's Commissioner

My local MP

The Justice Secretary

The Head of the GLC

The Home Office Minister

The Attorney General

MPs interested in Women's Rights from all parties

The Courts and levels:

1. **Magistrates' Court** - initial hearings. This is also where an appeal of sentence can take place. Usually appeals are only allowed after all of the list have been addressed: equivocal plea (not a clear guilty plea); an injustice; fresh evidence; mistakes that the police, CPS or courts have made in the process; or a unique situation (such as a global pandemic). Though I could prove each of the above, the court still stated that my application to appeal both my conviction and sentence was 'above their jurisdiction'.

2. **Crown Court** - level 2 hearings, with or without a jury. This is where an appeal of conviction and sentence is processed ie. To appeal 'everything' and an injustice. They decide whether they felt the Magistrates' Court made the right decision to convict you. They can also decide whether they felt you were pressured to change your plea by examining what legal advice you were told , whether you were pressurised and what were the circumstances. Despite

you having strong evidence, it is a high benchmark to achieve a result in your favour. In their eyes, you have already admitted, whether you wanted to, or not, whether you were coerced to or not and irrespective of whether the circumstances left you with no option, that you are, essentially, a criminal.

3. **The High Court at the Royal Courts of Justice** - who decide whether the Crown Court followed the correct process. It's useless to present evidence to this court, to show the initial accuser lied in his evidence as this will not be considered in their decision

4. **The Appeal Court at the Royal Courts of Justice**. This is where a clerk decides whether there is a point of law in your case to justify the courts spending time and money re-investigating your case.

5. **The Supreme Court** - who decide whether your case is of public interest and highlights a point of law to justify an appeal and to have it reopened.

6. Lastly the **CCRC** (Criminal Cases Review Commission) which is where the buck stops. This is the last resort.

Don't expect to get to 4 or 5, even if you had and have strong evidence and even if it's a matter of public interest. This is an extremely high hurdle to climb.

Remember, if people are trying to bring you down, it only means you are above them.

Milton Keynes UK
Ingram Content Group UK Ltd.
UKHW020255111023
430276UK00012BA/125